MONEY TALKS:

The Essential Mindset For Financial Success

Chris Raymonds

Copyright © 2014 by Chris Raymonds

All rights reserved. No part of this publication may be reproduced, distributed, or transmitted in any form or by any means, including photocopying, recording, or other electronic or mechanical methods, without the prior written permission of the publisher

Published in 2014 by Mondy Publishing Co.

Although the author has exhaustively researched all sources to ensure accuracy and completeness of the information contained in this book, we assume no responsibility for errors, inaccuracies, omissions, or any inconsistency herein. Any slights of people or organizations are unintentional.

Readers should use their own judgment and/or consult a financial expert for specific applications to their individual situations.

ABOUT THE AUTHOR

Chris Raymonds is a senior treasury analyst in one of the big-five banks in Canada, in which he specializes in treasury accounting applications that manage corporate treasury and balance sheet. He has applied the teachings written in this book and has investments ranging from stocks, funds, real estate and businesses, amongst which include a business in equestrian show-jumping horses. Chris has shown family, friends and co-workers that anybody can properly achieve financial freedom by simply sticking to the basics.

Table of Contents

WELCOME TO THE RACE	6
STAY OUT OF THE RACE!	9
FAST TRACK	13
SHAPING YOUR THOUGHTS	16
ASSETS AND LIABILITIES	22
LET MONEY WORK FOR YOU	26
MIND YOUR OWN BUSINESS	32
PAY YOURSELF 20% FIRST	36
INVEST IN THE MARKET	41
DOLLAR COST AVERAGING	49
START NOW	54

PREFACE

When it comes to finance, a lot of people don't know where to begin. The most important information about finance is usually expressed with too many numbers and formulas for a regular person to understand. Well-written articles are usually too dry and boring for a regular person to finish reading.

I believe that *Money Talks* is where you begin. It accomplishes what these things cannot by taking a "heart-to-heart discussion" approach to the teaching of finance. Money is talking to you in an enthusiastic and informative way that will teach you how simple financial planning ought to be.

After reading the book, I wish you are as excited as I still am about financial planning.

- *Chris Raymonds*

Hello there!

You probably know me already.
Why wouldn't you? You're addicted to me. You can't get enough of me. You wish you have more of me.

But do you really?
You work your butt off to get more of me, but somehow you always let me go.
You say you want me to grow, but somehow you cut me off right away.
You think I'm the answer to your problems, but somehow you end up with more.
You feel I will make you happy, but somehow you end up feeling worse.

Somehow, you don't know me at all!

I'm here to change all of that.
I will teach you how you should think.
I will teach you how I work.
And then, I will teach you how to sit back, and let me work for you.

All you have to do is follow me.

Compoundingly Yours,
Your Money

WELCOME TO THE RACE

Go to school.
Study hard.
Get good grades.
Find a good company to work for.
Then your life is finally set.

Does this sound familiar to you?

It should. These are the so-called "advice" people would tell you. Who can blame them? This is the safest route anybody can take, and it has worked throughout their lives.

The average person has a typical "life cycle". The person is born, grows up, then goes to school. He then shines in school, gets top grades and goes to a respectable college/university. He then graduates and finds a well paying job. After all, he's been working towards that goal all his life.

Once he gets a taste of money, he learns to enjoy his money: dining out, shopping, and going out on dates — worse, accumulating debt in credit cards.

Somewhere along the road, he finds the love of his life. They get married. They buy a house, a car, furniture, and start traveling for vacation.

As time goes by, they soon realize they need more money to keep up with their life. So naturally, they work harder — asking for promotions and raises. They work longer hours to keep their jobs. They study harder to build their skills so they become valuable and less likely to be laid off. As this happens, their tax bracket goes up. They pay more and more in taxes.

They decide it's time to raise a child. Therefore, they need a bigger house, which means their real estate tax goes up (paying more in taxes yet again!) and so does their mortgage.

Sounds familiar?

This person has become a Rat Racer, and is now stuck in vicious cycle called the Rat Race. The entire race has been to work for anybody else but himself — he works for someone's company to get a salary, for the government through taxes, and for the bank paying off mortgage and credit card debts.

The cycle gets worst as this exact process is then passed to their children as advice.

Welcome to the Rat Race… Ready. Set. Go! And, we're off!

STAY OUT OF THE RACE!

Have you felt you were never paid enough? Have you complained about paying so much taxes? Did you hate your boss for passing you over for promotion, or not giving you the well-deserved raise? Did you think it was unfair that you were laid off? Did you ever feel that life is unfair?

At any point in the Rat Race, you would have felt at least one of the things above.

"Life is unfair. It pushes all of us around. Deal with it!" Knowing that this remains a constant in life is crucial. It's how you work with this information that separates us from being rat racers for life. There are two things you can do:

1. Give up, do nothing, and let life push you around.
2. Fight! Learn the lesson that life is pushing you around to learn, and push back.

If you do #1, you live your life complaining about your job, your low pay, or your boss (or me!) for your problems.

If you do #2, good for you! This already shows you want to learn something. This is why you picked up this book anyway, right?

When you set your mind to what I share, you will become a financially successful person.

The best thing to do is to change the way you look at things. There's no point complaining about what's going on with your life, hoping that someone will come to change things and save you. You have to be the change you want to be. Be an agent of change. Do something! If there's a problem, change it. If you're the problem, change yourself. Either way, you will learn something and gain wisdom in the process.

When it comes to the topic about money, most people don't want to change. This is how they end up with a low paying job — a low pay is still better than no pay, which is risky. Then they end up blaming the company for abusing them, when, in fact, they are abusing themselves.

Not a lot of people want to learn how to have money work for them simply because it's easier to learn to work for money, especially if they fear the subject of money: fear of missed payments, fear of job loss, fear of not having enough, or fear of starting from scratch. This fear puts me in control of you instead of the other way around.

Most people can be bought because of fear and greed. First, they work hard because they fear losing money. Once they get a taste of money, they start thinking of all the things they can buy. That's when they get sucked into the race. Fear and greed start ruling their lives from then on.

The topic of money is a lifetime study because the more you learn, the more you realize how much you don't know... However, most people end their learning when they graduate from school.

Therefore, stay clear off the Rat Race and on to the Fast Track!

FAST TRACK

Financial education is the key to fast track your way out of the Rat Race. You need financial literacy to be rich — this takes flexibility, open-mindedness and willingness to learn. But once you gain this education, you will grow richer and richer!

Unfortunately, school is not the best source of knowledge for this. Most of what's being taught in school these days are subjects you will rarely use. Schools focus on skills that will make you a smart employee, but not a rich one. Did the derivative of *ln* help get you that job? Does it matter what the different types of plants are at work? This is why the world is filled with top-notch professionals, who got top grades in school, but are financially broke all their lives.

What should be taught in school is the subject of money. A lot of people have little or no knowledge of this subject. Of the people who do, most don't even know how to apply it in real life like accountants or bankers.

The most obvious thing to do is to learn a lot about how money really works and how to invest. In this way, you can find your dream job — the profession that you have wanted to do all your life not because of salary, work benefits or job security. You won't need to study for something you don't want to just because it's required for your job. You are free to do and learn what makes you happy.

Money brings some power. But financial education is even more powerful because it gives you power and control over me. If you know how I work, you can start making me grow. Money is everywhere as long as you know where to look.

Retiring rich and comfortably is easily achievable, especially if you start young. When it comes to money, time is your best friend. Therefore, the best time to start is always NOW.

In this book, I will shape your thoughts so you have the proper mindset to fast track your way out of the race.

SHAPING YOUR THOUGHTS

The first thing you have to do to accomplish your goals is to shape your thoughts and get your mind straight. Having the correct mindset is crucial in understanding, accepting, and applying what I'm telling you. The good news is the fact that you're reading this book already means you are ready to shape your mind!

When you were a kid and afraid of ghosts or monsters, your parents are likely to tell you: "It's all in your head". That's how powerful your mind is. It will make you believe and do things based on your thoughts.

The Poor usually, if not always, say "I'll never be rich." or "I'm not meant to be rich." And that mindset becomes a reality. The Rich refer to themselves as rich and say: "I'm rich!" or "I deserve to be rich." And so they are!

The power of your mind is tough to wrap yourselves around in, but it's clear that you need to be aware of what your thoughts are and how you express them. In the end, these thoughts are what will become reality.

So the very first step in getting rich is by shaping your thoughts!

A lot of people view money as a bad thing — that being rich is bad, and therefore wanting to be rich is bad. It's become a taboo subject to bring up and discuss. What people don't understand is that money is neither good nor bad. It is neutral. It has no interest, whatsoever, in you, your family, nor your country. It is emotionless and only deals with facts. Which is why you should never bring emotions into question when dealing with money. Otherwise, these emotions and feelings end up becoming obstacles to getting rich. Therefore, getting rich means you need to think the way money thinks because it is as straightforward as getting the facts right.

More money is not the answer to your problems. When people are given more money, they just end up with more debt.

Why? Because everyone, both poor or rich, has a fear of losing money. I have mentioned this earlier, so it goes to show how important this is. But ask yourself, is fear the problem here? Definitely not! As I said, everyone has that fear. So what's the issue? Why is there a difference between the rich and the poor? It's because of how they handle the fear — handle losing — handle failure. This makes the difference in one's life. The Poor, especially, are also afraid of finding out that they've been losing financially — that they have been spending more than earning, that they have to cutback and lose the lifestyle they are used to.

Michael Jordan, one of the greatest basketball

players in NBA history, said "I've missed more than 9000 shots in my career. I've lost almost 300 games. 26 times, I've been trusted to take the game winning shot and missed. I've failed over and over and over again in my life. And that is why I succeed."

And this is exactly how winners are different from losers. For winners, the secret to winning and success is that they draw inspiration and learning from their failures. Therefore, the fear of losing becomes an opportunity to win! That's why the Rich are rich. The Poor are losing financially because the fear of losing money outweighs the opportunity of being rich. The Rich accept failure as an opportunity so they grow smarter and stronger. They are not afraid to make mistakes. In terms of money, the Rich know that their financial failure is just a bump along the way to a greater financial success.

As you go through your financial journey, your mind needs to be more focused and stronger than ever. You will encounter all sorts of noise, both internal and external. Internal noise includes the fear and self-doubt creeping over you, making you think you won't be able to make it, or that you'll fail and never recover. Basically, it's the pessimist in you, thinking your are not good enough. External ones include loved ones, family or friends, who will be keen on pointing out your flaws, criticizing you, or explaining why you will not succeed or what you're doing is not the right course of action.

Most people end up poor because they listen to these noises. Since people don't have the proper mindset, the noises become very powerful and end up hitting them emotionally. But as I said, money is emotionless. This is why I emphasize the importance of shaping your thoughts. It's what will get you past the criticisms and noise. It's what will make you a winner instead of a loser. Focus on the facts. Winners analyze, opening their eyes; whereas, losers criticize, blinding them. As you progress, you will get to see things which losers were blind to — opportunities that they missed. And being able to find the missed opportunities is key to any success.

ASSETS AND LIABILITIES

The best way to spot opportunities is by knowing the difference between assets and liabilities. People struggle financially because they do not know the difference.

An asset is something that makes money for you. A liability is something that takes money away from you.

Therefore, a very simple rule out of basic knowledge: to be rich, simply buy assets.

Rat Racers feel the problem is not having enough money. But, really, the problem is where they spend their money on. The Rich buy assets. The Poor buy liabilities, but they think they are assets — which is the worst part of it all.

One of the biggest liability people fail to accept is

their home. Most people "invest" all their salary into this "asset" that they may never end up owning. All expenses spent on their homes like furniture, utilities, maintenance are all paid with after-tax dollars. Property taxes hit people even after paying off their mortgage. Houses do not necessarily appreciate in value so people even end up losing money. Worst of all, think of all the missed opportunities in investing in assets that could've made money for them. Since majority of their income is spent on their home, they may even have to work more just to keep up with the amount of expense the house is incurring, instead of building up their assets.

When people lose their jobs, that's when they realize that their home is not an asset at all, but a liability that keeps generating expenses. It still takes money for them every month as opposed to real assets that should be giving them money in this crucial time of job loss.

In the end, foregoing the opportunity to start an investment portfolio over the ownership of an expensive house results in the following losses:
- Time in which assets could've grown and made more money for you (see chapter: Let Money Work For You)
- Money in which you could've invested in more assets
- Learning in which the experience would've made you a better investor

We should always ensure that our assets are greater than our liabilities, and try our best to keep liabilities and expenses low. This is why the Rich get richer. Their income from assets cover their liabilities/expenses, with the excess being reinvested back into more assets. As their assets grow, the income from those assets grows along with it.

Examples of assets:
1. Stocks
2. Bonds

3. Mutual Funds

4. Businesses that can be left to run by itself

4. Rental income from real estate

5. Passive income from royalties for intellectual property

Shape Your Thoughts:

When planning on spending on liabilities/expenses, buy assets that will pay for them instead. This ensures your liabilities/expenses are always lower than your assets.

LET MONEY WORK FOR YOU

Abracadabra! Brace yourself for this chapter. This is where you'll learn how the magic happens: How you can be like the Rich — letting money work for you through their assets.

Let me ask you: If you put $10,000 in an investment that gives a yearly interest of 5%, how much money will you have after 20 years?

Is your answer $20,000?
Calculation: 5% of $10,000 is $500. In a span of 20 years, you will get $10,000 (20 years multiplied by $500 per year) plus the $10,000 you put in, making it a total of $20,000.

If this is your answer, then you are like most people — wrong!

The correct answer is $26,532.98 — that's a whooping $6,532.98 more than what most people think!

Isn't this magic? How did this happen? This is the magic of compounding, or compound interest.

Compounding is how you let money work for you. It works by adding the interest you have earned as part of the principal for succeeding interest calculations. Think of it as "interest on interests".

In our example above, let's break down how it worked:

You have put $10,000 in the savings account with 5% yearly interest.
At the end of the first year, you get $500 in interest — 5% of $10,000.
For the second year, most people think they will be getting $500 again from their $10,000.
However, this is where the mistake is and where

compound interest does its magic.

Since you received $500 interest in your first year, your money for the second year is now $10,500 instead of $10,000. Therefore, at the end of the second year, you will be getting $525 (5% of $10,500) instead of just $500.

This means that for the third year, you will be starting with $11,025 and the 5% interest at the end of the year will be $551.25.

This goes on and on until you decide to take out your money.

Table of compounding for first 10 years of the example:

Year	Principal	5% Interest	New Principal
1	10000.00	500.00	10500.00
2	10500.00	525.00	11025.00
3	11025.00	551.25	11576.25
4	11576.25	578.81	12155.06

5	12155.06	607.75	12762.82
6	12762.82	638.14	13400.96
7	13400.96	670.05	14071.00
8	14071.00	703.55	14774.55
9	14774.55	738.73	15513.28
10	15513.28	775.66	16288.95

Isn't this amazing? And it's so simple! All you have to do is set aside that money to work for you, then you just sit back and wait as it earns money for you. And the best part is, the money it earns is then used to earn money too! Compound interest is like a reward for leaving money alone to do its job.

As you can see with compounding, the longer it's left to compound, the more it grows. Time is such a big element in this magic. This is why it's best to start young since the money will have many years to compound and grow without doing anything. But like I said, the next best time to do this is NOW!

Just to give a view on how time makes such a big difference. Let's compare two scenarios:

Scenario 1: $10,000 growing at 5% interest for 30 years — three times the years of Scenario 2
Scenario 2: $30,000 growing at 5% interest for 10 years — three times the principal of Scenario 1

In Scenario 1, the $10,000 becomes $43,219.42 after 30 years.
In Scenario 2, the $30,000 becomes $48,866.84 after 10 years.

See how close Scenario 1 is from Scenario 2? That's how important time is when it comes to compounding, and why it's so much better to start when you're young. A smaller investment compounding for a longer time is usually better than a bigger investment compounding for a short time.

Once you set aside a dollar to work for you, never let

it come out. In this way, the principal still keeps compounding and you will be generating good interest income. Think of it as a business, your company: Once a dollar is in your business, it becomes your employee. It's in your best interest to keep the employees working to generate consistent profits. Once you start laying employees off, then you give up the profits generated by those employees. But if you follow this tip, then you maintain the same amount of profits, and the profits are all yours to use!

Shape Your Thoughts:
When making a purchase, imagine how much that money could grow through compounding. Is the purchase still worth it — losing the money that you would've made instead if you let it work for you?

MIND YOUR OWN BUSINESS

From the previous chapter, you learned to think of your assets as a business.

People struggle financially because they forget the difference between their profession and their business. Cooking in a restaurant is a profession. Owning the restaurant is a business. Since most people think the company they work for is their business, they end up minding somebody else's business for the rest of their lives and forget to mind their own. At the end of their working days, somebody else became rich, and they have nothing to show for their business.

Therefore, a rule to be rich is to start minding your own business.

Now that you know the difference between your

profession and business, here's a good strategy to be rich. Continue with your profession so you have a steady flow of income, but also mind your business by buying assets that will start making money for you.

Here's the secret when minding your business that ensure your road to riches: invest twenty percent (20%) of all the money you make for long term growth.

As an example: If you're making $30,000 per year, put $6,000 per year ($500 per month) in your business for the next 30 years. With an average of 6% return a year, you would end up with around $500,000!

Since you are saving a percentage of the money instead of a fixed amount, then this amount automatically adjusts when your salary changes. Because inflation makes sure things get more expensive, this is all the more reason to save and mind your business! This solution will help beat inflation through the magic of compounding.

Where did this 20% come from? From the very popular Pareto Principle! This principle is also called the 80-20 rule, which states that, almost with anything, 80% of the outcomes come from 20% of the inputs. For example, 20% of the business's customers account for 80% of the business's income. Applying this to "minding your business," it means that 20% of your income now will account for 80% of your retirement income. For the remaining 20% of retirement income, you will also have other sources of income like the government and company pensions.

Shape Your Thoughts:
As you continue your profession, always find ways to mind your business. This can be as simple as negotiating a salary increase, finding a better paying job, or looking for other sources of income like part-time jobs. The increase in income will

dramatically affect your business as 20% of it goes into your business.

PAY YOURSELF 20% FIRST

Now let's talk about saving the money first. At this point, you might be thinking to yourself: 20% is such a big amount of money! How will I be able to save that much? I have so many bills to pay, things to buy and a life to live.

People pay their bills every month. However, there is someone who is most important that they forget to pay - themselves. They will usually try to save what's left in their account after paying their bills and expenses. But this usually ends with no money being left at the end of the month for saving.

There's a simple and painless solution to that: Pay Yourself First! In this case, Pay Yourself 20% First! It's one of the best ways to be financially secure in retirement.

What this solution means is simple: take out the 20%

of the money right off your pay cheque or bank account, before you can even think of spending it.

The beauty of this solution is you'll barely even notice the money that disappeared. There might be some changes in your current standard of living, but it won't be anything dramatic. As a matter of fact, you'll see how easily your life will adapt to this change without noticing a difference. And since paying yourself first is going to be a fixed, regular and constant thing that happens with every money you make, your business will keep growing and the magic of compounding will take care of the rest.

Remember: Mind your business! Pay yourself first before you pay everybody else (this doesn't mean not paying them on time): the bank through mortgage, the credit card company through bills and the government through taxes. With technology, this has become so much easier. You can setup direct deposits from your pay cheque to a retirement account, or pre-authorized contributions (PAC) that automatically withdraw money from your bank account to a retirement account.

Don't pay your bills right away or when you receive the statement. Pay them as close as possible to make the actual date (since sometimes there is a delay in how long payment gets through to the billing company). You can use the payment money to work for you first before you actually need to pay the bill. Don't waste that opportunity!

Pay Yourself First has added bonuses in that it automatically shapes your thoughts mentally and financially through motivation. If ever you become financially short to pay bills because you paid yourself first, the creditors will come barking at your door. Therefore, you are forced to think of ways to come up with the money to pay them... or else! This "or else" becomes a motivation that makes you start thinking of other ways to make money: getting overtime pay, finding part-time jobs, starting a company — anything to avoid the dreaded "or else".

Even though it's not a good situation to be in, it's still better than having no pressure but being broke. Paying yourself first forces you to think of ways to make more money so you can pay everybody else. And the more money-making exercises you do, the stronger your money sense is.

You should never dip into savings to pay your bills. This is a bad habit that differentiates the Poor and Rich. Instead of finding ways to make money to pay the bill, the Poor usually take the lazy way out and just take money out of their savings to pay for their bills. The Rich know there are a multitude of ways to make money, and their savings should only be going straight into their business to make more money.

Shape Your Thoughts:
From now on, calculate your budget assuming you only have 80% of the money. The 20% should automatically be out of sight, out of mind, and in to your business! This ensures that the 20% will never

be used for anything other than making money for you.

INVEST IN THE MARKET

Now that you're able to set aside that 20%, you ask yourself: "Where should I put the money in?"

Most people would say to put it in stocks or in real estate.

If you don't know stock analysis, don't even bother with common stocks. It's a rough and tough game, where discipline is very crucial. To succeed in the game, you have to buy low, when everyone else is selling, and sell high, when everyone else is buying. Don't even bother with stockbrokers. They are just about as good as any random guy you get in the streets. A broker is an individual or party that performs transactions between a buyer and a seller. And that's exactly why they are called "stockbrokers", and not "stock analysts". Their job is to buy or sell stocks on your behalf, not to understand nor advice on them.

For a stock portfolio to be successful, you also need a well-diversified number of stocks in different industries so that you're not "putting all your eggs in one basket". Otherwise, if you invest only in one stock (company), then your entire investment purely depends on this company. If the company goes bankrupt, you've lost your investment. When you're just starting off, you will not be able to invest your 20% in a lot of different stocks (yet).

Real estate is also very expensive, which is why it's not a good place to use your 20%. You also need more time and effort to deal with any issues with the estate and with people like renters, lawyers, etc… Similar to common stocks, you need to have a good understanding of the housing market to succeed in this area. And like stockbrokers, real estate brokers are just there to help you buy or sell real estate. They do not necessarily know anything about the location nor housing market.

As you can see, investing in one-off stocks or real estate is not a good way to use your 20%. Take note, I said "one-off". Stocks and real estate are still great areas for investments. It's just that, for the 20%, I think the best way to invest, at least for people who can leave the money alone for several years, is to invest in the market, be it the stock market or real estate market.

How can someone invest in a market when I already said it's very costly and risky to invest in one-off stocks or real estate to begin with? Through investments called Mutual Funds.

A mutual fund is nothing more than a professionally managed pool of money. Basically, you and other like-minded investors put together your money and have a professional manage the money for you through investments like stocks, bonds, real estates, etc…

There are benefits to investing in Mutual Funds.

1. Professional money management - your money is being invested by someone who knows, or supposedly know, what he or she is doing.

2. Diversification - I mentioned that a successful portfolio needs to be diversified. With mutual funds, you are able to own shares in a wide range of investments.

3. Passive - these investments are hands-off. Since there is a professional managing the money for you, you don't need to do anything other than invest your money in the fund. Since most people have work, family or other things they need to do, they don't have time to look at their investments.

A carefully selected equity mutual fund gives you access to all of these. That's why it's the best way to put your 20%.

Like with any investment, mutual funds still have risks. There are no guaranteed income, and can be a roller coaster of ups and downs in price. If the market drops big, so will your mutual fund.

Equity funds are funds that invest in ownership securities like common stocks. They are very long term investments, at least 7 years. I said the stock market goes up and down a lot, but this is in the short term. And this is precisely why you should be thinking in the long term. One thing you should know is that, in the long term, the stock market always performs well.

Remember the first step to be rich was to shape your thoughts. You need to shape your thoughts that the stock market performs in the long term. This is very crucial because you will be tested in the toughest way. During the time your money is invested, you will see the market go up and down, and maybe even crash. Don't be scared and cash out when it goes down. Remember, the market performs well in the long run! Family or friends may persuade you to get out of the market. Remember, you're in this for the long term! You will make money in the long run regardless of the noise.

How will you make money? Mutual funds make money in three ways:
1. Capital Gains (Growth) - the fund makes a profit when it sells stocks at a higher price than it paid for.
2. Dividends - these are payments made by the company to shareholders, usually to distribute profits.
3. Interest - from other investments like bonds or cash.

At least once a year, the fund gives you back the profits as dividends.

Because of the dividends, it is important that you are enrolled in the Dividend Re-investment Plan (DRIP) for the fund. This plan will take any dividends from that fund and reinvests them in the form of additional shares. This is where you will see the magic of compounding take effect — the additional shares bought from your dividends will then start to give dividends as well. Most fund management companies enroll you to DRIP automatically, but it's good to make sure.

Now you can see that things are starting to fall into place. Mind your own business by paying yourself first with 20% of your income. Invest the 20% in mutual funds for the long term and see your money grow through compounding - any capital gain through price appreciation is a bonus!

Shape Your Thoughts:

If you have excess money you can set aside, then put it in mutual funds instead of leaving it at the bank. Remember, we shouldn't be dipping into our savings! Since mutual funds are less accessible and visible, we are not easily tempted to dip into it. It takes longer to get the money because you have to sell the shares and transfer the proceeds. Also, you will have to login to another account just to see how much you have (unless your investment account is with your bank).

DOLLAR COST AVERAGING

By now, you should have shaped your thoughts that the market performs in the long term. In the short term, it's like a roller coaster — heart-pumping excitement on the way up and gut-wrenching fear on the way down. But why should fear even be an option? Wouldn't it be better if it was all excitement?

Now you can get excited on the entire roller coaster ride! Say hello to the power of Dollar Cost Averaging! This second bit of magic, after compounding, makes the down times work to your advantage as well.

Dollar Cost Averaging is simply buying stocks or mutual funds at fixed intervals with a fixed dollar amount. You're probably still unsure how this makes down markets advantageous, right? It's best to show the magic with an extreme example:

Say you decide to save $100 a month and invest it in the MoneyTalks fund. The month you start your program, MoneyTalks is trading at $20 a share, so obviously you buy 5 shares ($100/$20 a share = 5 shares). The second month, MoneyTalks is trading $10, dropping by 50%... not good. Your $100 now buys you 10 shares. In month three, the fund has rebounded somewhat and now trades at $15, still well under your original purchase price. You buy 6 and 2/3 shares. So what's happening?

You'd think you've broken even. You're down $5 a share on your purchase at $20, you're up $5 share on your purchase at $10, and you're even on your final purchase.

You're wrong. You own 21 and 2/3 of shares. And how much are the shares currently worth? $15 each. What's 21.67 times $15? $325. How much did you invest in? $300! You're up $25 dollars in 3 months -

a great return in such a short period!

Because you're putting in a fixed amount each month, you obtain more shares at the lower prices. You bought 10 at $10, but only 5 at $20. Basically, it means that your average cost per share will be lower than the average price per share. In the long run, or even in the short run, that bodes well for the investor.

Table of Dollar Cost Averaging:

Month	Contribution	Fund Price	Number of Shares
1	100	20	5
2	100	10	10
3	100	15	6.67
Total Shares			21.67
Average Cost per Share ($300 / 43.33)			13.84

So one month when the stock market is struggling

and your mutual fund is suffering accordingly, don't let fear take over into cashing our your shares. Look at it as an opportunity to buy more shares at a good price! Dollar cost averaging is great stuff.

With the stock market, timing is another problem. It's very hard for anybody, amateur or professional, to time a purchase accurately — or even just to find time to do so. But if you buy in fixed intervals (e.g. buy every first day of the month), that's not a problem at all! And since you're buying continuously, you'll be buying high sometimes, but you'll also be buying low sometimes. With dollar cost averaging, you know this already works to your advantage.

The fact that you're in this for the long term isn't a problem, either. Since you're holding for at least 10 years, short-term market slumps, even prolonged ones, will work to your advantage instead.

So next time you hear people complaining about a

market slump, smile and realize that you're buying more shares at a cheaper price.

Remember paying yourself first? It has a magical relationship with Dollar Cost Averaging. The fixed interval you need for dollar cost averaging is already the same interval when you pay yourself first. See how easy it is? Now that you believe that dollar cost averaging works, forget discipline, courage, intelligence and an eye for value. You don't need any of them. You buy shares every pay cheque.

Shape Your Thoughts:
It's best to buy mutual funds and stocks, once you get into them, that gives dividends. They already accomplish everything I have been teaching you. They are assets because they make money for your (one of which is thru dividends). The dividends give the compounding effect. And since dividends are a given on a fixed interval (monthly, quarterly, semi-annually or annually), they automatically do dollar cost averaging!

START NOW

By now, you should have the proper mindset on managing your money.

To save you time in the future in case you need a refresher, here's a quick summary of the essential mindset for financial success to save you time from re-reading the entire book again.

1. Financial education is never ending so keep shaping your thoughts!
2. Buy assets, not liabilities. Assets make money for you and can make even more by compounding.
3. Mind your own business by finding ways to buy more assets.
4. With any income you make, pay yourself 20% first to buy assets.
5. The market performs in the long run. Invest in them.
6. Stop worrying about the short term. Buy assets at

fixed interval to achieve dollar cost averaging.

It's now time to set yourself out and apply what you've learned. Remember, time is your best friend when it comes to money. So start now, and I'll see you in your retirement!

www.ingramcontent.com/pod-product-compliance
Lightning Source LLC
Chambersburg PA
CBHW051821170526
45167CB00005B/2102